To my parents, who always answer when I call home. You're still my favorite people.
—S. M.

To Perseverance—I hope you can make it further on the adventure that Oppy started.
To Art, who's always there to bring humor and support for me on my adventures.
—C. L.

Text copyright © 2022 Shaelyn McDaniel
Illustrations copyright © 2022 Cornelia Li

First published in 2022 by Page Street Kids
an imprint of
Page Street Publishing Co.
27 Congress Street, Suite 1511
Salem, MA 01970
www.pagestreetpublishing.com

Distributed by Macmillan, sales in Canada by The Canadian Manda Group

22 23 24 25 26 CCO 5 4 3 2 1
ISBN-13: 978-1-64567-469-6
ISBN-10: 1-64567-469-X

CIP data for this book is available from the Library of Congress.

This book was typeset in Colby. The illustrations were done digitally. Cover and book design by Melia Parsloe for Page Street Kids. Edited by Courtney Burke and Kayla Tostevin for Page Street Kids.

Printed and bound in Shenzhen, Guangdong, China

Page Street Publishing uses only materials from suppliers who are committed to responsible and sustainable forest management.

Page Street Publishing protects our planet by donating to nonprofits like The Trustees, which focuses on local land conservation.

Bibliography and further info available at this link:

**Hello Opportunity | Pagestreet**
www.pagestreetpublishing.com

# HELLO, OPPORTUNITY

## The Story of Our Friend on Mars

**Shaelyn McDaniel**     illustrated by **Cornelia Li**

PAGE STREET KiDS

A long time ago, humans looked up at the wide blue sky and said, "We want to go there."

So we did.

Next, we looked up at the big white moon and said, "We want to go there."

So we did.

Then we looked up farther, past the sky, past the moon, to a little red planet named Mars and said, "We want to go there."

But we still had work to do, and the little red planet was too far away. So we sent a friend instead.

We made her, putting her together piece by piece—nine eyes, three ears, one arm, six wheels, and metal skin all the way around. She was a good shape for a friend and an even better shape for an explorer.

We named our friend Opportunity, which means "a good chance" and feels like hope. And since we were friends, we gave her a nickname—Oppy.

Oppy left Earth on a warm July evening, riding a rocket into the sky with a **woosh** and a *phwoom*. We watched until she was out of sight, hidden in the stars.

It was a long trip. As Oppy's rocket traveled, Earth traveled, too, around the sun from summer to winter. The new year came, and with it, a new celebration.

Oppy's rocket had made it to Mars. She landed with a bounce,

**ONE**

**TWO**

**THREE**

**FOUR**

We cheered. She rolled. We roared. Finally, Oppy's lander stopped, and she looked out for the first time. We whooped and hugged.

Then she made her first phone call home.

>HELLO, OPPORTUNITY!

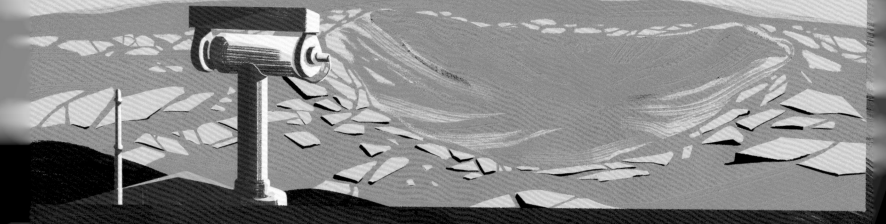

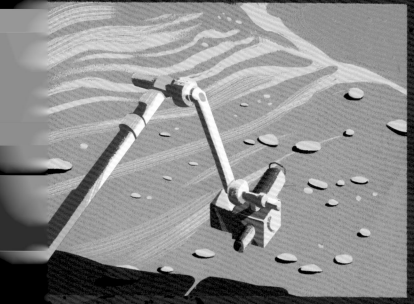

The little red planet had many secrets to discover and mysteries to solve. Oppy's new home was dry and empty, but maybe it hadn't always been. Maybe, once upon a time, there had been water. Maybe there had been life.

>SET A NEW DRIVING RECORD TODAY--140 METERS (459.3 FEET).

>GOOD JOB, OPPORTUNITY!

Oppy's job was to be a bold scientist, a brave adventurer, and a clever detective. Her special eyes were like a magnifying glass, searching for clues. She could look and see the little red planet for what it was and what it had been, like a storybook told in tiny pieces. Here, little round pebbles that whispered of running water. There, layers left in the dirt from a long-gone sea. Everywhere, new and exciting surprises.

Oppy called home often, and we were always happy to hear from her. Sometimes she sent selfies so we would know she was okay. Sometimes she sent photos of her new world that took our breath away.

It was long, hard work discovering the secrets of the little red planet. Sometimes the trip was scary and even dangerous. The little red planet was a long way from a tow truck if Oppy got stuck or a repair shop if something broke, but she kept going, and we helped when we could.

>HAVE DUG INTO SOFT DUNE MATERIAL, IMPEDING FURTHER PROGRESS.

>TRY ROLLING BACKWARD.

Oppy was supposed to stay on the little red planet for three months. Instead, she stayed for fifteen years. We kept in touch the entire time, watching our friend as she traveled the planet's surface.

But then, a storm came.

The storm covered Oppy in darkness and dust. The sun couldn't reach her batteries, and her energy drained.

It was time to say goodbye. We sent her one last message, a love song, a lullaby, a kiss from her friends on Earth.

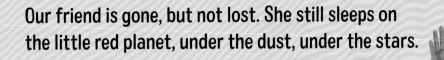

Our friend is gone, but not lost. She still sleeps on the little red planet, under the dust, under the stars.

ne day, the little red planet won't seem
o far.

e humans will follow our hope. We will
sit the little red planet for the first time.
e will wake our friend.

# OPPORTUNITY'S MISSION

- July 7, 2003 Mars Rover Opportunity (MER-1) is launched.
- January 24, 2004 Opportunity lands on Mars.
- March 2004 NASA announces that Opportunity and her sister rover Spirit have found further proof of history of water on Mars, including evidence of a shallow, salty sea.
- May 2004 Opportunity takes panorama of Endurance Crater.
- December 2004 Opportunity takes panoramic selfie on Mars.
- April 26, 2005 Opportunity gets trapped in a sand dune, nearly dooms mission.
- June 6, 2005 NASA announces that Opportunity is free, back to traveling again.
- June 10, 2018 Last communication from Opportunity received by NASA's Space Flight Operations Facility.
- February 12, 2019 Last attempt made to wake up Opportunity by playing "I'll Be Seeing You," sung by Billie Holiday.
- February 13, 2019 Opportunity's mission is officially declared complete.
- March 5, 2020 NASA's new Mars rover, Perseverance, is christened after a public contest.
- July 30, 2020 Mars Rover Perseverance launches.
- 2022 European Space Agency's ExoMars rover to launch.

Thirteen visitors have landed on Mars so far:
- VIKING 1 and 2 in 1976 (landers)
- PATHFINDER and SOJOURNER in 1996 (lander and rover)
- MARS POLAR LANDER in 1999
- SPIRIT and OPPORTUNITY in 2004 (rovers)
- PHOENIX in 2008 (lander)
- CURIOSITY in 2012 (rover)
- INSIGHT in 2018 (lander)
- PERSEVERANCE, MARS-A, and TIANWEN-1 in 2021 (rovers and rover/lander)

Oppy's work looked at the past, present, and future. Oppy took readings of the planet's clouds and dust, studied the way the atmosphere worked, and watched how her solar panels were affected. This information, combined with the many years of practical experience driving a rover on another planet, will help future missions.

Two months after Oppy's final message, NASA created a portal on their website where fans from all around the world could send digital postcards to the rover to encourage her to wake up. You can still read them online.

# A SNAPSHOT OF OPPORTUNITY

Four of Oppy's cameras are up top. The big ones on either side are her panoramic cameras, which help her drivers decide where to go next. The smaller, inner cameras are her navigation cameras, which show how to get to the next spot.

These flat pieces aren't wings. They're solar panels! Opportunity uses the sun's energy to go, go, go.

Opportunity is just under five feet tall, so when scientists back home look through her eyes, they can look at Mars from a grown human's height.

There's a small rectangle of metal on Opportunity made from the debris of the demolished World Trade Center towers. This rectangle protects the cables that make Opportunity's drill work.

Her other cameras are mostly on her arm, with one on the back of her head. Instead of taking photos or navigating, these are special instruments that allow Oppy to study the planet itself, looking on scales and wavelengths that normal cameras—and human eyes—can't see.

Each of Oppy's six wheels has its own motor so they can move independently of each other.

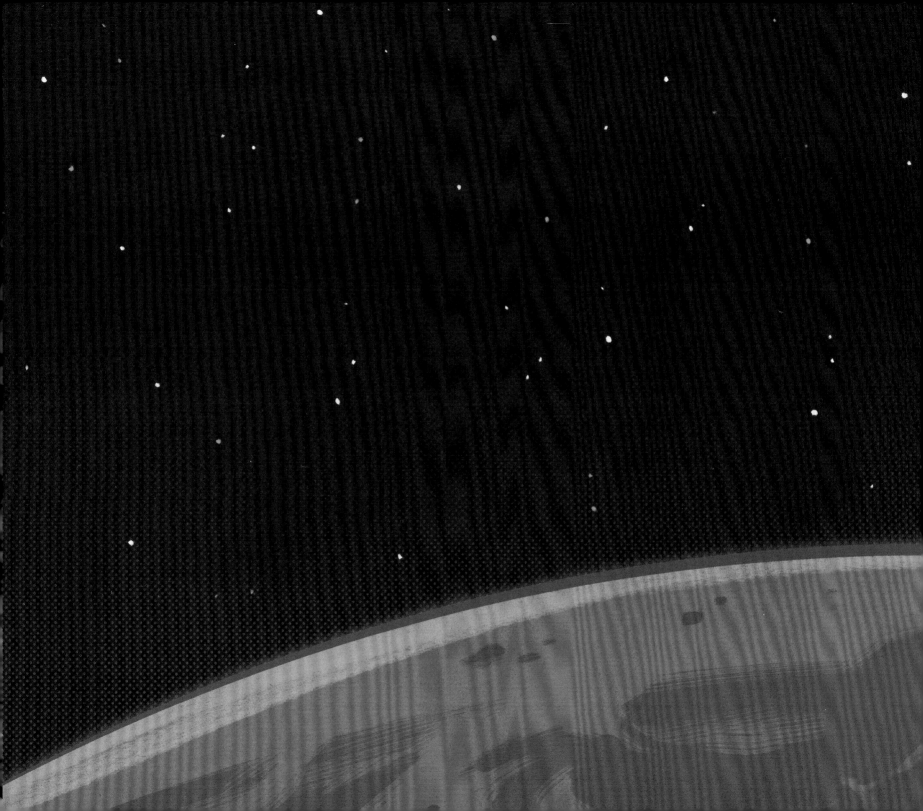